A Guide for Using

The View from Saturday

in the Classroom

Based on the novel written by E. L. Konigsburg

*This guide written by **Colleen Dabnev***

Teacher Created Resources, Inc.
6421 Industry Way
Westminster, CA 92683
www.teachercreated.com
ISBN: 978-1-57690-348-3
©1999 Teacher Created Resources, Inc.
Reprinted, 2008
Made in U.S.A.

Illustrated by
Agi Palinay

Edited by
Jennifer Overend Prior, M.Ed.

Cover Art by
Wendy Chang

Table of Contents

Introduction

A good book can touch our lives like a good friend. Within its pages are words and characters that can inspire us to achieve our highest ideals. We can turn to it for companionship, recreation, comfort, and guidance. It can also give us a cherished story to hold in our hearts forever.

In *Literature Units* great care has been taken to select books that are sure to become good friends!

Teachers who use this unit will find the following features to supplement their own valuable ideas.

- Sample Lesson Plans
- Pre-reading Activities
- A Biographical Sketch and Picture of the Author
- A Book Summary
- Vocabulary Lists and Vocabulary Activity Ideas
- Chapters grouped for study with each section including:

    —*quizzes*
    —*hands-on projects*
    —*cooperative-learning activities*
    —*cross-curricular connections*
    —*extensions into the reader's own life*

- Post-reading Activities

- Book Report Ideas

- Research Activity

- Culminating Activities

- Three Different Options for Unit Tests

- Bibliography of Related Reading

- Answer Key

We are confident this unit will be a valuable addition to your planning and we hope your students increase the circle of "friends" they have in books as you use our ideas.

Sample Lesson Plans

Each of the lessons suggested below can take from one to several days to complete.

Lesson 1
- Introduce and complete some or all of the pre-reading activities found on page 5.
- Read "About the Author." (page 6)
- Read the book summary. (page 7)
- Introduce the vocabulary list for Section 1. (page 8)

Lesson 2
- Read Chapter 1. As you read, place the vocabulary words in the context of the story and discuss their meanings.
- Choose a vocabulary activity. (page 9)
- Construct a "B & B Thank-You Note." (page 11)
- Start a "Classy Classroom Scrapbook." (page 12)
- Be a "Smart Shopper." (page 13)
- Begin "Reading Response Journals." (page 14)
- Administer the Section 1 quiz. (page 10)
- Introduce the vocabulary list for Section 2. (page 8)

Lesson 3
- Read Chapter 2. Place the vocabulary words in context and discuss their meanings.
- Choose a vocabulary activity. (page 9)
- Make rugelach. (page 16)
- Explore the art of pantomime. (page 17)
- Learn about sea turtles. (page 18)
- Do "What's Cool at School." (page 19)
- Administer the Section 2 quiz. (page 15)
- Introduce the vocabulary list for Section 3. (page 8)

Lesson 4
- Read Chapter 3. Place the vocabulary words in context and discuss their meanings.
- Do a vocabulary activity. (page 9)
- Complete "Penny for Your Thoughts." (page 21)
- Do "What's Your Cup of Tea?" (page 22)
- Research famous women in history. (page 23)
- Discover your genealogy. (page 24)

- Administer the Section 3 quiz. (page 20)
- Introduce the vocabulary list for Section 4. (page 8)

Lesson 5
- Read Chapters 4 and 5. Place the vocabulary words in context and discuss their meanings.
- Do a vocabulary activity. (page 9)
- Design art for "The Gallery." (page 26)
- Do "The Choice Is Yours." (page 27)
- Complete "Simply Similes." (page 28)
- Search for kind acts. (page 29)
- Administer the Section 4 quiz. (page 25)
- Introduce the vocabulary list for Section 5. (page 8)

Lesson 6
- Read Chapters 6–12. Place the vocabulary words in context and discuss their meanings.
- Do a vocabulary activity. (page 9)
- Complete "Can You Solve the Puzzle?" (page 31)
- Learn about acronyms, initials, and abbreviations. (page 32)
- Complete "A Jumble of Jobs." (page 33)
- Complete "Watch for Signs." (page 34)
- Administer the Section 5 quiz. (page 30)

Lesson 7
- Discuss any questions your students have about the story. (page 35)
- Assign the book report and research activity. (pages 36 and 37)
- Begin work on one or more culminating activities. (pages 38–41)

Lesson 8
- Administer Unit Tests: 1, 2, and/or 3. (pages 42, 43, and 44)
- Discuss the test answers and possibilities.
- Discuss the students' enjoyment of the book.
- Provide a list of related reading for your students. (page 45)

Before the Book

Before you begin reading *The View from Saturday* with your students, do some pre-reading activities with the class to stimulate their interest and enhance their comprehension. Here are a few activities and discussion questions that might work for your class.

1. Predict what the story might be about just by hearing the title.
2. Discuss with students how their daily routines differ on Saturday in comparison to other days of the week.
3. Ask the students about other books by E. L. Konigsburg that they might have read.
4. What challenges might someone have to face going to a new school?
5. Is it "cool" to be smart? Explain.
6. Name various ways we can help someone who is different from ourselves feel welcome in the classroom.
7. What contests or competitions have you entered in school or outside of school?
8. What are some techniques for developing good teacher-student relationships?
9. When the odds are against you to succeed at something, what character qualities does it take to be a winner?
10. Have students fold an 8 ½" x 11" piece of paper in half horizontally then in half again vertically. This will make four rectangles when unfolded. Instruct students to sketch one activity in each space depicting what they do on Saturdays. Use these pictures on a bulletin board entitled "Our View from Saturday." Post other projects related to the book as the students complete them.

About the Author

E. L. (Elaine Lobl) Konigsburg was born in New York, New York, on February 10, 1930. Her father was a businessman named Adolph Lobl and her mother's name was Beulah Klein. Konigsburg, along with her two sisters, was raised in the mill towns of Pennsylvania. Konigsburg read a lot and drew pictures as a child. She was an excellent student, graduating as the valedictorian from Farrell High School. No one in her family had gone to college, and she knew nothing about scholarships, so Konigsburg planned to work her way through school. She worked odd jobs while in college, such as being a playground instructor, waitress, and library page. Being a chemistry major and spending many hours in the lab left Konigsburg little time for her artistic endeavors. Her friends never knew that she could draw and write.

After graduating with honors, she married David Konigsburg, an industrial psychologist. Next, she went on to graduate school. The Konigsburgs relocated to Jacksonville, Florida, where she began teaching science at a private girls' school. In 1955, Konigsburg's teaching career was placed on hold when she began having children of her own.

In 1962, Konigsburg moved back to New York. She began exploring galleries, museums, and New York City. Her writing career soon began to blossom. In 1968, she won the Newbery Medal for her first book, *Jennifer, Hecate, Macbeth, William McKinley, and Me* . Her second book, *From the Mixed Up Files of Mrs. Basil E. Frankweiler* was the Newbery runner-up that same year. No other author has had that honor. Konigsburg illustrated her earlier books using her three children as models. Her grandchildren have modeled for her more recent picture-book illustrations.

Konigsburg usually spends between a year and a year and a half writing a book. She writes and rewrites many times and doesn't send a book to the publisher until it's exactly the way she wants it to be. She believes that children's books need to have "a certain kind of excellence." While she wants them to appear nonchalant and easy, she also wants them to be based on good writing techniques and accurate history.

Konigsburg has received numerous awards and honors for her books. *The View from Saturday* won the 1997 Newbery Award for excellence in children's literature. In addition to being an excellent writer, E. L. Konigsburg loves painting, reading, gardening, and chocolate! She and her husband, David, live in Ponte Vedra Beach, Florida. Her writing studio overlooks the Atlantic Ocean, and she often gets ideas for novels by beachcombing. You can write her at the following address:

E. L. Konigsburg
c/o Atheneum Publishers
866 Third Avenue
New York, NY 10022

The View from Saturday

by *E. L. Konigsburg*

(Antheneum, 1996)

(available in Canada from Distican; UK, Simon & Schuster; AUS, Prentice Hall)

The View From Saturday is a story about four sixth graders who are selected for an academic team called "The Souls." Noah Gershom, Nadia Diamondstein, Ethan Draper, and Julian Singh, under the direction of their teacher, Mrs. Olinski, beat the seventh grade team at their school, Epiphany Middle School. Then they beat the eighth grade team and finally go on to win the district and regional championships.

The Souls emerge as both team and individual champions by overcoming personal obstacles. Noah Gershom remembers being stuck at a retirement community called Century Village in Florida when most kids his age would be off at Sea World or Disney World. While visiting his grandparents, he meets unique people and even gets to be best man in a wedding.

Nadia Diamondstein has to adjust to dividing her time between her mom's home in New York and her dad's home in Florida. She visits her dad and spends her time struggling to communicate with her father and others about her parents' decision to live apart. She finally looks beyond her own problems and finds a greater mission in rescuing sea turtles off the coast of Florida.

While indifference would be an easy solution for Ethan Potter as he sees classmates show unkindness towards both a strange kid in town and a handicapped teacher, he chooses instead to be a catalyst for good by encouraging and befriending those who are different from himself.

On Saturdays, Noah, Nadia, and Ethan meet with the fourth member of the Souls, Julian Singh, at his father's bed and breakfast home called Sillington House. The Souls practice questions for their academic bowls and drink tea together. Julian finds true friendship among the group which helps to heal the wounds from the torment he endures at the hands of other students on the bus and at school.

E. L. Konigsburg's *The View from Saturday* portrays characters similar to those you'd encounter right in your own neighborhood. These characters are sure to be endearing. This book will leave you wanting to see the Souls take on more contests and challenges in the future.

Vocabulary Lists

On this page are the vocabulary lists which correspond to each sectional grouping of chapters. Vocabulary activities can be found on page 9 of this book.

Section 1
(Chapter 1)

superintendent	benevolently	pareve	rabbi
puberty	bated	brisket	canopy
brawn	nibs	ironic	dirigibles
decorum	domiciles		

Section 2
(Chapter 2)

onyx	multiculturalism	mammoth	tolerant	frazzled
coiffed	incandescently	hybrid	sarcasm	meddling
diversity	atrociously	subtle	pathetic	philosophical
cherubs	Yiddish			

Section 3
(Chapter 3)

nonchalantly	knoll	chanteuse
suffragette	paraplegic	incubating
archive	clones	hybrid
itinerant		

Section 4
(Chapters 4 and 5)

spontaneous	acronym	tranquilizer	dignity
suppressed	carafe	laymen	ruckus
admonish	matinee	domestic	genius

Section 5
(Chapters 6–12)

trounce	translucence	Koran	parched
culled	ethnicity	Upanishads	sovereign
vanquished	anemia	audible	perpetual
trajectory	converged	photosynthesis	malice
jubilant	phalanx	frieze	audible
stealth	unison	patrons	blitz
capacity	reincarnation	sentinels	unprecedented
caryatids	incarnation		

Vocabulary Activity Ideas

You can help your students learn and retain the vocabulary in *The View from Saturday* by providing them with engaging vocabulary activities. Here are a few ideas to try:

- People of all ages like to make and solve puzzles. Ask your students to make their own **Crossword Puzzles** or **Word Search Puzzles** using the vocabulary from the story.

- Challenge your students to a **Vocabulary Bee!** This is similar to a spelling bee, but in addition to spelling each word correctly, the game participants must correctly define the words as well.

- **Play Password.** Divide the class into two teams. Pick one person from each team to sit facing away from the board. Write a vocabulary word on the board for the other team members to see. Students should alternate giving one-word clues until one of the teammates in the chairs guesses the word. Allow a thirty-second time limit for a response. Keep score by awarding ten points for a correct response on the first clue, nine points on the second clue, etc.

- As a group activity, have students create an **Illustrated Dictionary** of vocabulary words.

- Play **Vocabulary Concentration.** The goal of this game is to match vocabulary words with their definitions. Divide the class into groups of 2–5 students. Have students make two sets of cards the same size and color. On one set of cards write the vocabulary words and on the other set write the definitions. All the cards are shuffled and placed facedown on the table. A player picks two cards. If the selection is a match, the player keeps the cards and takes another turn. If the cards do not match, they are returned to the table, and another player takes a turn. Players must be attentive to the placement of the words and definitions. This is a great activity for a learning center.

- Play **Vocabulary Charades**. In this game vocabulary words are acted out.

- Draw a **Tick-Tack-Toe** grid on the board. Divide the class into two teams. Call out a vocabulary word to a team member. If that person gives the correct definition, instruct him to place an "X" or an "O" on the grid. If he gives an incorrect response, give that same word to the opposing team. Continue alternating team players until one team gets three X's or O's in a row on the grid.

- Have your students practice their writing skills by creating sentences and paragraphs in which several vocabulary words are used correctly. Ask them to share their **Compact Vocabulary** sentences and paragraphs with the class.

You probably have more ideas to add to this list. Try them! See students' vocabulary interest and knowledge increase.

Quiz Time

Read each question carefully and answer on the lines provided.

1. Where was the bowl game held? _____

   _____

2. What two teams were competing for the championship? _____

   _____

3. What is a B & B letter? _____

   _____

4. What did Tillie's cat, T. S., do? _____

   _____

5. Tell how each person was going to help at the Diamondstein wedding. _____

   Mr. Cantor _____

   Tillie _____

   Mrs. Kerchmer _____

   Grandma Sadie_____

   Rabbi Friedman _____

   Bella Dubinsky _____

6. What happened to Allen Diamondstein and how did Noah get to be best man? _____

   _____

7. Name the gifts given for the specially marked invitations._____

   _____

   _____

8. How did the gifts keep on giving? _____

   _____

9. How was Century Village so unlike Disney World or Sea World? _____

   _____

   _____

10. Do you think Noah was disappointed about his visit to Grandma Sadie and Grandpa Nate's
    house? Why or why not? _____

    _____

    _____

B & B Thank-You Note

Noah Gershom's mother insisted that he write a B & B letter to his grandparents. Noah didn't think he owed them one. He couldn't think of much to be thankful for, and when he requested to use the computer, his mother's response was, "Write!" Eventually, he took out his pen and calligraphy paper and began.

Think about the many workers at your school who work day after day with little praise or recognition. Brainstorm, as a class, to discuss who these valuable workers are and list them on the board. The list might include the janitor, school nurse, librarian, cafeteria workers, office workers, or your classroom parent volunteers.

Have each student design a thank-you card for one of the workers listed. Use crayons, markers, glue, construction paper, sample wallpaper books, and other paper scraps to design the cards. The students should write short thank-you notes in appreciation of what these school helpers do to make the school a better place.

Remind students to proofread their cards to make sure all words are spelled correctly. Also, make sure they sign their cards. Provide time for the class to make special deliveries of their cards to their school's very special workers.

Before you begin your card, ask yourself the following questions:

1. What does this person do to make our school a nice environment?

2. How has this person helped me?

3. What items could I draw on the card that would please this person?

Next, use the sample card below to draft your thank-you note. Proofread and edit your card and then make the final copy.

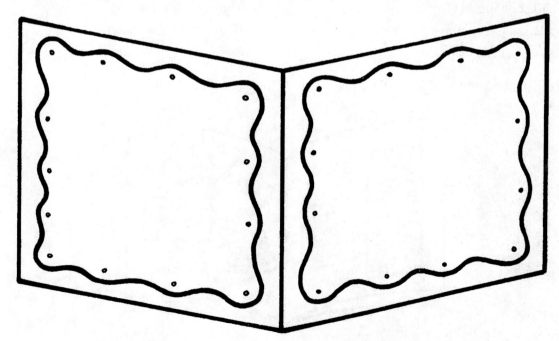

Classy Classroom Scrapbook

Memorable events happen at Epiphany Middle School. We can record classroom occasions in a lasting way by creating a classroom scrapbook. To do this, divide your students into five groups. Assign each group one of the following topics: Fun Field Trips, Awesome Awards, Art Projects and Activities, Everyday Happenings, and Special Visitors and Programs. Ask parents to donate film or money to help defray the cost of film development throughout the year.

What You Need:

1. a store-bought scrapbook with removable pages
2. classroom photos
3. camera and film
4. stickers
5. paper edgers
6. colored paper
7. acid-free markers for journals

Have students capture important events on film for scrapbook photos. Provide time for students to summarize the events and to write photo captions. Students should work in groups to collaborate on page layout. Watch wonderful memories unfold event by event. Keep the scrapbook on display for parents and other people who visit your classroom. At the end of the year, let each student have his or her favorite page as a special keepsake.

With a little variety, this project can serve as an ongoing history project as well. Have students think about a place they have fond memories of visiting, just as Century Village made a lasting impression on Noah. Using construction paper, magazines, used postcards, pamphlets, etc., have each student design a page about his or her favorite location. Research additional geographical information by using the encyclopedias, the Internet, or other available resources.

You might want to include some of the following items:

1. A map showing the location
2. Population, size, climate of the location
3. Interesting facts or people
4. Things to do, events
5. History of the location

Title the finished compilation of all the kids' work, "Our Classroom Gazetteer!"

Smart Shoppers

Century Village residents go shopping for the Diamondstein wedding. Below are some of the items they need for the reception. Circle the item in each square that would be the most economical to buy. Do comparison shopping the next time you are in the grocery store. Use newspaper ads, coupons, and a calculator to figure out how to get the most for your money. Write a paragraph summary of your findings.

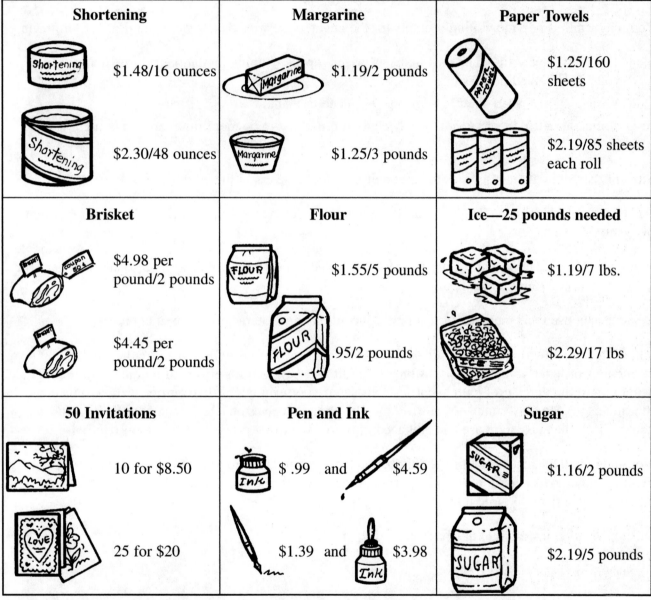

Shortening	Margarine	Paper Towels
$1.48/16 ounces	$1.19/2 pounds	$1.25/160 sheets
$2.30/48 ounces	$1.25/3 pounds	$2.19/85 sheets each roll

Brisket	Flour	Ice—25 pounds needed
$4.98 per pound/2 pounds	$1.55/5 pounds	$1.19/7 lbs.
$4.45 per pound/2 pounds	.95/2 pounds	$2.29/17 lbs

50 Invitations	Pen and Ink	Sugar
10 for $8.50	$ .99 and $4.59	$1.16/2 pounds
25 for $20	$1.39 and $3.98	$2.19/5 pounds

Sample Problem: Find the per unit price of each item by dividing.

Post-It Notes

ultra colors 100 sheets

$7.73/pk.

$$100\overline{)7.73} \quad .0773$$

$$\begin{array}{r} .0773 \\ 100\overline{)7.73} \\ \underline{70} \\ 73 \\ \underline{70} \\ 3 \end{array}$$

Recycled Post-It Notes

50 sheets

$1.18/pk.

$$\begin{array}{r} .0236 \\ 50\overline{)1.1800} \\ \underline{1\,00} \\ 180 \\ \underline{150} \\ 300 \\ \underline{300} \end{array}$$

Reading Response Journals

One great way to ensure that the reading of *The View from Saturday* becomes a personal experience for each student is to include the use of Reading Response Journals in your plans. In these journals, students are encouraged to respond to the story in a number of ways. Here are a few ideas:

Ask students to bring in inexpensive, one-subject notebooks for their journals. Tell students that the purpose of the journals is to record their thoughts, ideas, observations, and questions as they read.

You may want to provide writing prompts for the chapters. Three ideas for chapter 1 are the following:

1. Noah gave away five cherished items as prizes for the winning invitations. Write about five of your most valued possessions.
2. Write a short B & B letter to someone you need to thank.
3. Tell about a trip or place you have been that turned out to be more fun than you thought it was going to be.

Students can draw their responses to certain events or characters in the story.

After reading each chapter, students can write what they learned by summarizing the important events in the story.

The journal could be used as a diary for personal reflection on the story or as a personal dictionary for unfamiliar words found in the text.

Students can use their journals for mapping concepts such as characterization, main ideas, or theme.

Allow students to write in their journals daily. Personal reflections will be read by the teacher, but no corrections or letter grades will be assigned. Credit will be given for effort. If a grade is desired, grade according to the number of journal entries completed. For example, if five entries were assigned and the student responsibly completes all five, then he or she receives an "A." As an alternative, students could select one entry to revise and edit according to the writing process. Score the final revision.

Non-judgmental teacher notations should be made as you read the journals to let students know you are reading and enjoying their journals. Here are some types of responses that will please your students and encourage them to write more.

"You have good insight into this passage."

"Your writing is so clear, I feel as if I am there."

"You seem to be learning a lot from this book and showing the ability to apply it to your life."

Quiz Time

Read each question carefully and answer on the lines provided.

1. How did the Souls affect Mrs. Olinski? _____

   _____

2. What reason did Mrs. Olinski give Dr. Rohmer for choosing the four members of her academic team? _____

   _____

3. When Nadia visited her dad, what didn't she like him to do? _____

   _____

   _____

4. What happened when Nadia phoned her former friends?_____

   _____

   _____

5. What relationship brings Nadia the most satisfaction? _____

   _____

   _____

6. What brought Izzy and Margaret together? _____

   _____

   _____

7. How is Margaret different from Bubbe, Izzy's first wife? _____

   _____

8. How was the ticket problem for *The Phantom of the Opera* solved? _____

   _____

   _____

9. Why was Nadia upset with Margaret? _____

   _____

   _____

10. How were Nadia and her dad's trip plans changed? _____

    _____

Really Delicious Rugelach

In chapter two, we learn that Margaret Draper Diamondstein is nothing like Nadia's grandmother, "Bubbe." Nadia said, "Bubbe would have had homemade rugelach. Margaret did not even know what rugelach were until Grandpa Izzy took her to a kosher delicatessen and introduced her to them." Have you ever tried these bite-size cookies? Classic rugelach is sure to be a class treat!

Classic Rugelach (makes 32 rugelach)

Dough

- 4 oz. (100 g) cream cheese, softened
- $\frac{1}{3}$ cup (80 ml) unsalted butter, softened
- $\frac{1}{4}$ cup (60 ml) packed light-brown sugar
- $\frac{1}{2}$ tsp. (2.5 ml) salt
- yolk from 1 large egg
- 1 $\frac{1}{2}$ (360 ml) cups unsifted all-purpose flour

Filling

- 1 cup (240 ml) finely chopped walnuts or hazelnuts
- $\frac{1}{3}$ cup (80 ml) packed light-brown sugar
- $\frac{1}{4}$ tsp. (1.25 ml) cinnamon
- 2 tbsp. (30 ml) honey

Glaze

- White from 1 large egg, lightly beaten
- 1$\frac{1}{2}$ tbsp. (22.5 ml) granulated sugar

Directions:

Dough: In large bowl with electric mixer on medium speed, beat cream cheese, butter, brown sugar, salt, and egg yolk until light and fluffy. On low speed, beat in flour until just combined. Divide dough in half. On lightly floured surface, shape each half into $\frac{1}{2}$" (1.3 cm) thick disk; wrap disks separately in plastic wrap. Place in refrigerator to chill at least 2 hours or overnight. Preheat oven to 350° F.

Filling: In bowl, combine nuts, brown sugar, and cinnamon; stir in honey. On floured surface, roll 1 dough disk to 10$\frac{1}{2}$" (27 cm) round; trim to an even 10" (25 cm) round; lightly press onto dough to adhere. Cut into 16 wedges. With spatula, slide one wedge out from round. Start at wide end; roll up toward point. Roll up remaining wedges. Place cookies point side down on nonstick baking sheet (or regular sheet lined with parchment paper).

Glaze: Brush cookies with egg white; sprinkle with sugar. Bake 16 minutes, until lightly browned. Let cool on rack. Repeat with remaining dough, filling, and glaze. Store in airtight container.

Three more favorites

Pistachio-Cherry: Prepare dough as directed. Spread each round with $\frac{1}{4}$ cup (60 ml) cherry jam or preserves, large pieces chopped; sprinkle each with 3 tablespoons (45ml) chopped pistachios. Proceed as directed, sprinkling on additional pistachios with the sugar.

Double Apricot: Prepare dough as directed. Heat $\frac{1}{2}$ cup (120ml) strained apricot preserves and $\frac{1}{3}$ cup (80 ml) finely chopped dried apricots in saucepan until just simmering; let cool. Spread over dough rounds. Proceed as directed.

Chocolate-Coconut: Prepare dough as directed. In food processor, combine 1$\frac{1}{2}$ cups (360 ml) sweetened flaked coconut with 3 tablespoon (15 ml) sugar; process until finely chopped. Add 1 large egg white; process to blend. Spread over dough rounds; top each with $\frac{1}{4}$ cup (60 ml) finely chopped macadamia nuts and 1 ounce (28 g) chopped bittersweet chocolate. Proceed as directed.

Pantomime: The Art of Silence

While talking to Nadia Diamondstein, Ethan says, "We Potters make an art of silence" (page 46). When actors make an art of silence, it could be called "pantomime." Pantomime is acting without words. The word "pantomime" means "all mimic" in Greek. This type of acting began in ancient Rome where one dancer would use masks and costumes to play an assortment of characters.

In cooperative learning groups, practice pantomiming various emotions displayed by the characters in the book. Have students begin with just facial expressions and then graduate to more challenging whole-body moves. The students should refer to the actual scenes in the book for important details in their performances.

Pantomiming Possibilities

1. T. S., Tillie's cat, pouncing on Noah (Chapter 1)
2. Allen Diamondstein hovering over Nadia (Chapter 2)
3. Nadia calling her former friends (Chapter 2)
4. Nadia poolside with Ethan, Izzy, and Margaret (Chapter 2)
5. Allen Diamondstein calling for extra tickets for the opera (Chapter 2)

Scenes

1. Placing the cake on the ice (Chapter 1)
2. Tripping over the wagon handle (Chapter 1)
3. Noah writing his B & B letter (Chapter 1)
4. Grandpa Izzy digging out the nest (Chapter 2)
5. Driving in the rain to rescue the turtles (Chapter 2)

Future Scenes

1. Ethan seeing Julian and Mr. Singh for the first time (Chapter 3)
2. Julian standing at the board with the word "cripple" written on it Chapter 3)
3. The four Souls getting clues for the tea party (Chapter 3)
4. Shopping for Julian's gift (Chapter 3)
5. Overhearing the conversation on the bus (Chapter 4)

After several practices, groups should pick their favorite pantomimes to perform in front of the class.

Facts About Sea Turtles

Margaret Draper met Izzy Diamondstein by inviting him to join her on a turtle walk. The Diamondsteins, Nadia's grandparents, devote much of their time to protecting the turtles off the Florida coast. Margaret's enthusiasm inspires others to become involved in this cause. Nadia has learned about Florida turtles by doing a report.

Before reading chapter two, use the chart below to fill in what you already know about sea turtles. As you read chapter two, write down information you learn from the book. In the third column, write down questions you have about sea turtles and use the final column for information you find from research. Make sure you label your references to document your findings.

What I Know	What I Found in the Book	Questions I Have	Research, Facts, and Documentation

After the chart has been filled in, divide the class into five groups to do further research on the following sea turtles: loggerheads, greens, leatherbacks, hawksbill, Atlantic ridley.

What's Cool at School

There are many pertinent issues in *The View from Saturday*. Some of these issues include cultural diversity, treatment of the handicapped, and environmental protection.

Divide the class into three groups to discuss ways your school makes positive advancements in each of these areas. Have the groups list their findings in the appropriate columns on the chart below. After allowing ample time, have the groups collaborate their findings. Spend some time in discussion on ways your school could improve in each of these areas.

Have the class draft a letter of recommendation to the student council, principal, or other appropriate school officials. You could also do this project by analyzing your entire community. Students could then draft a letter to the editor of their local paper.

Cultural Diversity	Handicapped Treatment	Environmental Issues

Quiz Time

Read each question carefully. Answer in complete sentences.

1. What was the unwritten rule on the bus? _____
   _____

2. What did Ethan think of his brother? _____
   _____

3. What strange things did Ethan first notice about Julian? _____
   _____
   _____

4. What did Ethan like about Nadia? _____
   _____

5. Do you think Julian wrote "cripple" on the board? Why or why not? _____
   _____

6. How were the other students mean to Julian? _____
   _____

7. How did Julian react to the pressure? _____
   _____

8. What was Ethan's dream? _____
   _____

9. What responsibility did Ethan have on Saturdays with his mom? _____
   _____

10. How did Julian invite people to his party? _____
    _____

11. How did Nadia get to name the group? _____
    _____

12. Do you think the name fits the group? Why or why not? _____
    _____

13. Tell what each of the Souls wanted to relive.

Noah _____
_____

Nadia _____
_____

Ethan _____
_____

Julian _____

Penny for Your Thoughts

Each of the Souls held a shiny new penny minted in the year they became a team. They would slip each other a penny to signal an emergency gathering. Pennies have a portrait of Abraham Lincoln on the "heads" side and a picture of the Lincoln Memorial on the "tails" side. The Lincoln Memorial is an important landmark located in Washington, D.C. The cornerstone for this memorial was set in 1915 and the building was dedicated in 1922.

In *The View from Saturday*, Sillington House was the oldest farmhouse in Clarion County. Research nine famous landmarks and points of interest in your area. Find dates and detailed information by using resources in your library. Write the landmarks and dates on the fronts of the nine pennies below. On the backside write a short summary of each place. When all the pennies have been filled in, cut them out. Use the penny cards to practice learning important information about points of interest in your area.

What's Your Cup of Tea?

Noah Gershom

Nadia Diamondstein

Julian Singh

Mrs. Olinski

Ethan Potter

Directions: Each quality below matches one main character. Fill in each teacup with three selections for each person.

British accent	wears glasses	plump
blonde hair	cautious about being friendly	wears shorts and knee socks
black hair	best man in wedding	has a dog named Ginger
teacher	red hair	dreams of theater work
paraplegic	has a brother named Lucas	teaches calligraphy

Author's reveal characters in four ways: what the character says, what the character does, what others say about the character, and through narration. In small groups of two to five, compare answers, adding the characteristics and descriptions you know about each character. In your groups, decide which character would be the most interesting as a member of your classroom. Share group findings with the entire class.

Famous Women

The commissioner of education asked if a team member could name the famous women in American history associated with four places in New York. Ethan knew them all. How many names do you recognize below? Choose four names and research how each woman made a valuable contribution to our society. Fill in the spaces of the quilt squares with the five w's of informative writing—who the person is, where the person is from, when the person lived, what he or she accomplished, and why the person is famous.

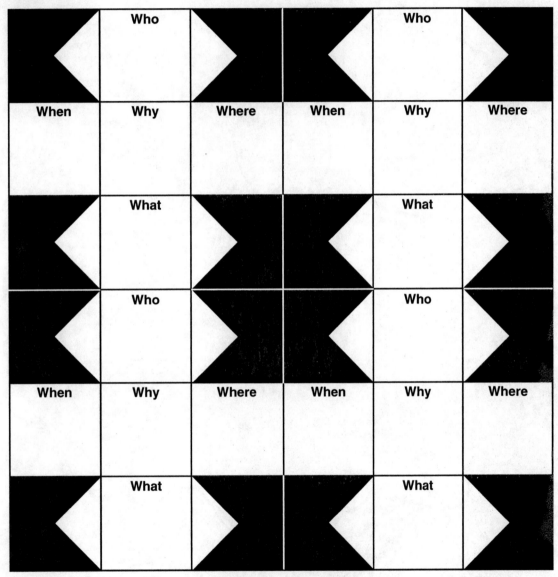

Word Bank

Marian Anderson	Shirley Chisholm	Rosa Parks
Susan B. Anthony	Amelia Earhart	Eleanor Roosevelt
Clara Barton	Geraldine Ferraro	Betsy Ross
Elizabeth Blackwell	Christa McAuliffe	Harriet Tubman
Pearl S. Buck	Sandra Day O'Connor	Babe Didrikson Zaharias

My Family Tree

Ethan had an historical record of his ancestors in the Clarion County Museum. What about you? Find out all you can about your family and fill in the names of your ancestors on the family tree below. (Add apples as needed.) Prepare an informative speech of three to five minutes about your genealogy to share with the class. Bring in photos or other family items that would make your talk more interesting.

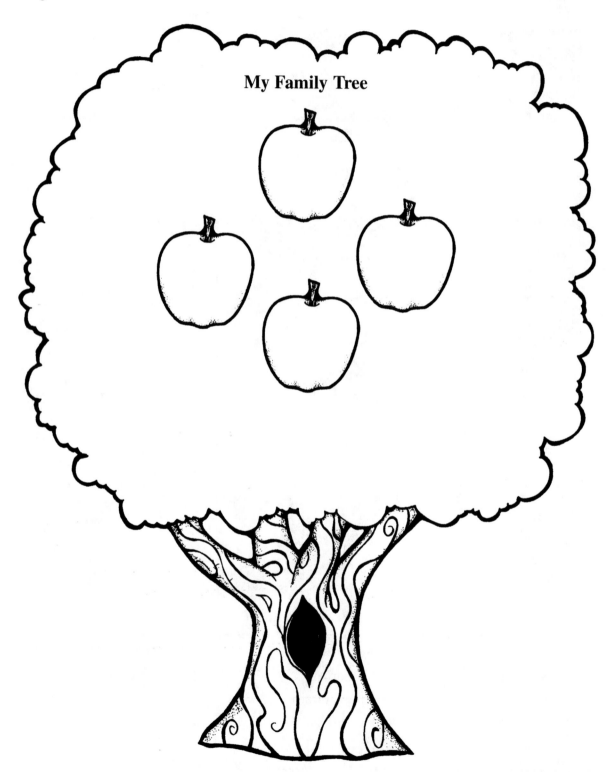

My Family Tree

Quiz Time

Directions: Read each question carefully and then answer with complete sentences.

1. For what play were the Souls training Ginger?_____

   _____

2. Why did Julian want Ginger to have the part? _____

   _____

   _____

3. What was Ham planning to do to Ginger, and how was the plan discovered? _____

   _____

   _____

   _____

4. How did the Souls signal each other that they wanted to talk? _____

   _____

5. How did Julian subtly show Ham that his trick had failed? _____

   _____

6. Why do you think that the Souls were not willing to reveal their association? _____

   _____

   _____

7. What challenge does Mrs. Olinski face with the other teachers? _____

   _____

8. Who did Mrs. Olinski seriously consider for the fourth spot on the team? _____

   _____

9. Mrs. Olinski had a tolerance for mischief, but she had no patience for malice. Explain._____

   _____

   _____

   _____

10. What impression did the Souls drinking tea together have on Mrs. Olinski? _____

   _____

11. What characteristics did Mrs. Olinski see in Julian that made her hesitant to choose him for the
    team? _____

   _____

The Gallery

Sometimes an author leaves the appearance of a character up to the reader's imagination. Other times these attributes are clearly described. In small groups, skim *The View from Saturday,* and on a separate sheet of paper, list the physical characteristics that are given for each person or place below. Next, use the list to individually draw your view of each character and place in each frame provided. You may want to use colored pencils or markers. Place completed pictures on a classroom bulletin board entitled "Our View of Konigsburg's *The View from Saturday.*"

The Choice Is Yours

Directions: Read each statement carefully. Discuss the statements in small groups. Decide if you strongly agree, agree, or disagree. Circle your choice and then explain your reasoning on the back of this page.

1. "There are times in school when a person had to do things fast, cheap, and without character." (Chapter 1)

   Strongly Agree   **Agree**   **Disagree**

2. "Many friendships are born and maintained for purely geographical reasons." (Chapter 2)

   Strongly Agree   **Agree**   **Disagree**

3. "When grandmothers disapprove of grandsons, it is usually their hair. Their hair or their music." (Chapter 2)

   Strongly Agree   **Agree**   **Disagree**

4. "Not answering the phone but hearing what people on the other end were saying was a little like spying." (Chapter 2)

   Strongly Agree   **Agree**   **Disagree**

5. "Gazing and listening are all right for church, but they sure kill a lot of conversations." (Chapter 3)

   Strongly Agree   **Agree**   **Disagree**

6. "An English accent makes...people seem more intelligent than they maybe are." (Chapter 3)

   Strongly Agree   **Agree**   **Disagree**

7. "Sixth graders had changed." (Chapter 4)

   Strongly Agree   **Agree**   **Disagree**

8. "It would have been better if Arnold had been eliminated altogether." (Chapter 4)

   Strongly Agree   **Agree**   **Disagree**

9. "...sometimes to be successful you have to risk making mistakes." (Chapter 5)

   Strongly Agree   **Agree**   **Disagree**

10. "There is a playful quality to mischief." (Chapter 5)

   Strongly Agree   **Agree**   **Disagree**

Simply Similes

Directions: Several examples of similes are found in *The View from Saturday*. Eleven are listed below. A simile is a comparison using *like* or *as*. Read each example and then rewrite the simile twice. First, change the comparison without changing the meaning of the simile. Then, change the comparison and give the passage the opposite meaning from what was originally intended. Use the back of this page if necessary.

1. "Dad hovered over me like a Goodyear blimp." (Chapter 2) _____

    _____

2. "...eyes are bright blue like the sudden underside of a bird wing." (Chapter 2) _____

    _____

3. "...she is thick around the middle, and when she wears her green polyester pantsuit, she looks like a Granny Smith apple." (Chapter 2) _____

    _____

    _____

4. "He watched as patiently as a cameraman from National Geographic." (Chapter 2) _____

    _____

    _____

5. "...it seemed as exciting as watching a red light change." (Chapter 2) _____

    _____

    _____

6. "Mother avoids the subdivision as if it were a toxic waste dump." (Chapter 3) _____

    _____

    _____

7. "As American as apple pie." (Chapter 3) _____

    _____

8. "We had them (heavy hangers of polished wood) all facing the same way so that their shadows on the wall looked like a computer rendering of an architectural cross section." (Chapter 4) _____

    _____

9. "I answered by nodding my head like one of those nodding animals that Americans put on their rear ledge of their automobiles." (Chapter 4) _____

    _____

    _____

10. "Like the cursor on a computer screen, her eyes moved from the first row to the second, then stopped." (Chapter 5) _____

    _____

11. "...his wrists hanging below his cuffs like meter sticks showing how much he had grown..." (Chapter 5) _____

    _____

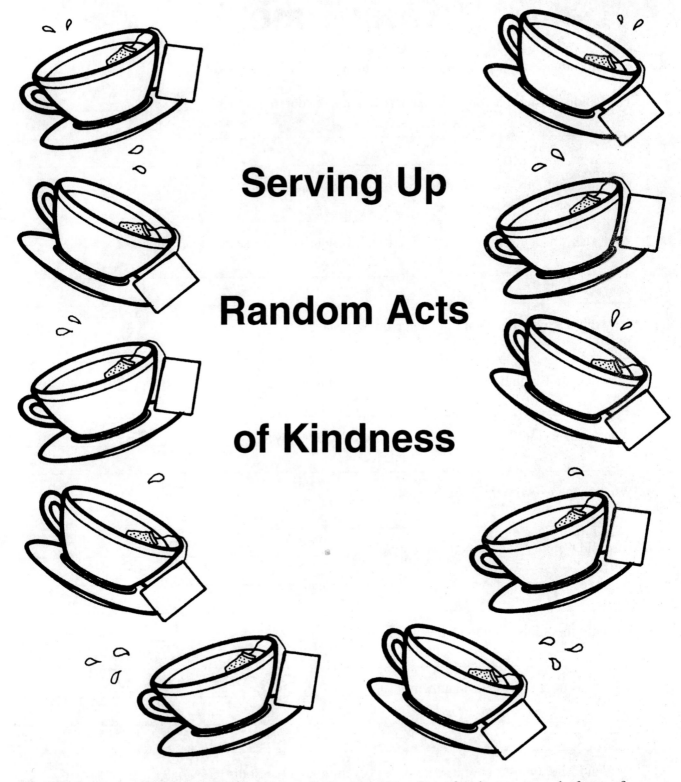

Serving Up

Random Acts

of Kindness

Directions: As you read through the chapters of *The View from Saturday*, keep a record of acts of kindness demonstrated by the main characters. Write a character's name on each tea cup. The page numbers where the information is located should be placed on the tea bags. As an extension activity, keep track of random kind acts within the classroom. Designate a location where students can put slips of paper with the names of classmates who do nice things. At the end of the week, talk as a class about each act of kindness. Have little rewards for these students. If desired, put students' names on construction-paper teacups for a bulletin-board display.

Quiz Time

Read each question carefully. Answer in full sentences on the lines provided.

1. The validity of what acronym was confusing for the commissioner? _____

_____

_____

2. How did the Souls give new meaning to the term "bottoms up"? _____

_____

3. What risk was Dr. Rohmer taking in letting Mr. Fairbain be master of ceremonies? _____

_____

_____

4. Why did the team not want to practice on Saturday? _____

_____

5. How did Mr. Singh destroy Mrs. Olinski's relaxed feeling? _____

_____

6. What category did Noah think was not necessary to study? _____

_____

7. What happened with the TV coverage? _____

_____

8. How did Century Village help out the Souls? _____

_____

_____

9. How did the Souls want to receive the trophy? _____

_____

10. What was the trophy called and why? _____

_____

_____

11. Why did Mrs. Olinski have a sense of loss even though the Souls had won? _____

_____

_____

Can You Solve the Puzzle?

The Souls were good problem solvers. Many times Noah, Nadia, Ethan, and Julian were faced with challenging questions to answer. They also enjoyed puzzles and creative thinking. Look at the picture puzzles below. Each piece represents a word or word phrase used in *The View from Saturday*, (chapters 6 through 12). Try to solve the puzzles together in cooperative learning groups or do the puzzles individually. After you have finished, try to design some puzzles of your own from other parts of the book to share with the class. Draw these on the back of your paper.

1. Wonder Alice Land	2. Bottoms	3.	4. after
5. o'clock o'clock o'clock o'clock	6. wins / losses	7. taken out	8.
9. High	10. CREDIT	11. Reasons Reasons	12. act
13. Show	14. Loss + + + + +	15. Sil ence	16. qu—es—ti—on
17. VisINible	18. grade grade grade grade grade grade grade grade	19. admission	20. CarnaREtion

Acronyms, Initials, and Abbreviations

When the commissioner asked the school teams to name two examples of acronyms that we use as words in our language, Julian responded with "posh" and "tip." This sent the advisory panel searching the computer and books to verify his response.

Thirty abbreviations, initials, and acronyms are listed below. Abbreviations are shortened forms of words, initials are first letters of words, and acronyms are words formed from initial letters of a series of words such as RADAR (Radio Detecting And Ranging).

Work in small groups to decipher the shortened forms of words below. Use the dictionary if you need help. Write your responses on the blanks provided. Sometimes there is more than one correct answer. When you have finished, challenge another team to answer five of your own.

AKA	_____	**HS**	_____
AP	_____	**MADD**	_____
APO	_____	**NASA**	_____
AIDS	_____	**NBA**	_____
BSA	_____	**PGA**	_____
CIA	_____	**POSH**	_____
CD	_____	**P.S.**	_____
CPR	_____	**PTA**	_____
DDS	_____	**SAT**	_____
EXT.	_____	**UPC**	_____
E-MAIL	_____	**UPI**	_____
ESL	_____	**WPM**	_____
FBI	_____	**WW**	_____
FDA	_____	**WWW**	_____
GED	_____	**XS**	_____

A Jumble of Jobs

Directions: *The View from Saturday* includes people from many walks of life. Match each person listed below with his or her occupation. Write the correct letter in the blank.

_____ 1. Mrs. Laurencin	A.	artist
_____ 2. Mr. Singh	B.	veterinarian
_____ 3. Dr. Gershom	C.	bus driver
_____ 4. Mrs. Gershom	D.	district superintendent
_____ 5. Noah's grandparents	E.	drama teacher
_____ 6. Bella Dubinsky	F.	bookkeeper
_____ 7. Mr. Cantor	G.	chef/inn owner
_____ 8. Mrs. Olinski	H.	accountant
_____ 9. Dr. Pat Knapp	I.	retired elementary school principal
_____ 10. Gopal	J.	real estate salesperson
_____ 11. Mrs. Korshak	K.	magician
_____ 12. Dr. Roy Clayton Rohmer	L.	dentist
_____ 13. Margaret Draper Diamondstein	M.	middle school principal
_____ 14. Mrs. Reynolds	N.	retired postman
_____ 15. Allen Diamondstein	O.	owned a bakery
_____ 16. Tillie Nachman	P.	sixth grade teacher
_____ 17. Holly Blackwell	Q.	anchorwoman

Extension: Survey the class as to occupations represented by the students' families. Try to arrange for parents with interesting occupations to be guest speakers in the classroom. Hold a discussion to find out the goals students have for themselves. Point out how current academics will help prepare them for long-term goals. Seek out free materials about occupations from your local employment commission.

Watch for Signs

When the Academic Bowl finals in Albany were over, Mrs. Olinski, Mr. Singh, and Julian traveled along the interstate back home to Epiphany. The word "epiphany" means a sudden, striking understanding of something. Each main character in *The View from Saturday* experiences a personal "epiphany." Mentally travel back through the book and decide what important lessons and changes each main character learned about themselves. Write a one-paragraph summary of your ideas for each main character. Conclude by summarizing how you have changed and what you will remember most from reading this Newbery Award-winning book.

Mrs. Olinski

_____

_____

_____

Noah Gershom

_____

_____

_____

Nadia Diamondstein

_____

_____

_____

Ethan Potter

_____

_____

_____

Julian Singh

_____

_____

_____

Me

_____

_____

_____

_____

Any Questions?

When you finished *The View from Saturday*, did you have some questions that were left unanswered? Write them here.

_____

_____

_____

_____

_____

Now work in groups or by yourself to prepare possible answers for the questions you asked above or those printed below. Give reasons for your answers. When you finish, share your ideas with the class.

- Do you think the Souls will continue to meet for tea even though the competitions are over?
- Will Mrs. Olinski coach a different team next year?
- Do you think Julian was embarrassed about his dad meeting him at the bus?
- Will Mr. Singh's Sillington House B & B become successful?
- Are Ham and Michael going to continue to plot tricks to play against others?
- Do you think Mrs. Olinski will gain the respect of other teachers?
- Will Margaret gain Nadia's love and respect?
- Will Nadia's relationship with her dad continue to improve?
- Do you think Ethan will ever let Nadia know that he likes the way the sunlight makes a halo of her hair?
- Will Mr. Singh let Julian keep Alice even though she barks at guests?
- Do you think Ham ever faces any consequences for his plot to drug Ginger?
- How does Mr. Singh have so much insight into the Souls?
- Do you think Mrs. Olinski regretted returning to teaching?
- What other goals will the Souls set for themselves?
- Knowing some of the Souls' talents, what can you see them doing as adults?
- What made the Souls such a good team?
- How would the Souls have failed if Hamilton had been selected instead of Julian?
- Do you think the Souls stay friends beyond Epiphany Middle School?

Book Report Ideas

There are numerous ways to report on a book once you have read it. After you have finished reading *The View from Saturday*, choose one method of reporting on it that interests you. It may be a way your teacher suggests, an idea of your own, or one of the ways mentioned below.

- **Game Time**

  Make a board game based on the story. Be sure to include instructions for how to play, use of the game board, and all the pieces necessary to play the game. This could be done in pairs.

- **It's No Secret**

  Choose one main character and seven important events from the book involving this character. Write diary entries, in paragraph form, from the character's point of view.

- **Walk Down Memory Lane**

  Choose at least five items that relate to *The View from Saturday* to put in a box or bag. These items can reflect the setting, theme, a character, or a specific scene. On 3" x 5" cards, write the significance of each item and share these in an oral presentation to the class.

- **Into the Future**

  Write a report that predicts what might happen if *The View from Saturday* were to continue. It may take the form of a story in narrative, a dramatization, or a visual display.

- **Come to Life!**

  This is one report that lends itself to a group project. A size-appropriate group prepares a scene from the story for dramatization, acts it out, and relates the significance of the scene to the entire book. Use costumes and props to will add to the dramatization.

- **Compare and Contrast Poster**

  Using poster board, make a poster comparing and contrasting your school to the school in the book. Enhance your poster with colorful drawings.

- **It's Comical**

  Design a comic strip to accompany the book. Choose three episodes in the book that appealed to you and illustrate them in comic form. Include "balloons" for characters' conversations and thoughts.

- **Literary Interview**

  This report is done in pairs. One student pretends to be a character in the story, immersed completely in the personality of his or her character. The other student plays the role of a television or radio interviewer, trying to provide the audience with insights into the character's personality and life. It is the responsibility of the partners to create meaningful dialogue.

Research Activity

Lifetime experiences helped the Souls, collectively, to have a vast knowledge of diverse topics. When opportunities for travel or learning present themselves, we should use these opportunities to expand our knowledge and interests. While we can't always travel to every place we want to know about, through reading and research we can learn things we never imagined.

Work in small groups to research fully one of the areas mentioned below or one of your own ideas. Share your findings with the class in an oral presentation.

People

- John Adams
- Susan B. Anthony
- Paul Bunyan
- Lewis Carroll
- Davy Crockett
- Ponce de Leon
- Martin Luther
- Native American leaders—
  Sequoyah, Tecumseh, Osceola, Geronimo
- Raphael
- Rembrandt
- Harriet Tubman
- George Washington

Places

- Florida
- New York
- Sargasso Sea
- Sea World
- Walt Disney World

General Topics

- academic contests for students
- *Annie*
- calligraphy
- dog intelligence
- Jewish foods, customs, and holidays
- magic tricks
- *The Phantom of the Opera*
- sea turtles—
  loggerheads, greens, leatherbacks, hawksbill, Atlantic ridley
- Underground Railroad
- Women's Rights

Host a Classroom Tea Party

Celebrate the completion of *The View from Saturday* by hosting a classroom tea party. Prior to the party, divide the class into the following committees. Each committee should elect a chairperson. Have each committee brainstorm ideas and decide on their responsibilities for the party. Meet as a class to make final decisions on party details. List the chairperson and members below.

	Chair	**Members**
Food (menu)		
Decorations		
Invitations		
Setup		
Activities and Entertainment		
Clean-up		

Give each committee the following list of questions to answer.

Food Committee (Menu)—What should we eat? What kind(s) of tea should be served? How will we pay for the food? Should we ask parents to bring in items? What foods were eaten at Sillington House? How much food is needed? How will we keep the water warm for the tea?

Decorations Committee—How should we decorate? What utensils and dishes do we need? Should we make party favors to remember the party?

Invitations—Who should we invite (grandparents, parents, another class, other)? On what date should we have the party? What time should we have it? Do we want to make the invitations or buy them?

Setup—Do we have enough tables and chairs? Does the furniture need to be rearranged?

Activities and Entertainment—Should we plan to have drama activities to portray actions in the book? Where should we display projects and activities that are complete? Is there someone who will take pictures? Do we know someone who collects tea sets or someone who runs a B & B who would be a guest speaker? Do we want to have a puzzle race by having two small identical puzzles and two teams race each other putting them together? What other ideas would be fun for entertainment?

Clean-up—Where are the necessary supplies for cleanup?

Have a fun tea party!!!

Knowledge Bowl

To practice for the finals in the Academic Bowl, the Souls made up questions on cards for a Jeopardy quiz contest. Use the cards on page 40 to develop a similar classroom game. The cards can help students prepare for tests, or the cards can be used in a general trivia-type game. Fifteen sample questions are located on the final pages of *The View from Saturday*.

Preparation for Play:
1. Cut out the cards.
2. Give each student a card and assign him or her a question category. Have each student write the category and a question in that category on the front of the card. The answer to the question should be written on the back. Categories used in *The View from Saturday* are science, history, the Bible, art, math, and English.
3. Point out to students that the cards are scored from 10 (being the easiest) through 50 (being the most difficult).
4. Remind students to write legibly.
5. An alternative to #2 would be to assign complete categories to cooperative learning groups for designing questions. Remember during game time that a team would be excluded from answering questions for the category in which it developed questions.
6. Write down a final question separate from the other questions.

How to Play:
Game A
1. Put all the questions into a bowl. Put a bonus star on any two questions. This will designate a double point value if answered correctly.
2. Divide the class into two teams.
3. Randomly select questions from the bowl for each student to answer.
4. If the question is answered incorrectly, give the opposing team the option to answer that question or they may select another card. If they select another card, return the missed question to the bowl.
5. When all the questions are answered, or at an allotted time, total the scores. Allow teams to wager points for a final Knowledge Bowl question. They may wager any number of points up to their total. Tell them the category of the question and have them submit on paper the points they are wagering. Call out the final question and let the students on individual teams work together to write down the answer to the question.

Game B
1. Write all categories on the board and underneath each category list the points 10, 20, 30, 40, and 50.
2. Arrange the questions in the same order on a desk or table.
3. Students can select a category of their choice and the difficulty level. As questions are answered correctly, erase them from the board.
4. Pre-select two questions that will count for double points.
5. Play continues as How to play # 4–5.

Knowledge Bowl Cards

10	20	30	40	50
10	20	30	40	50
10	20	30	40	50
10	20	30	40	50
10	20	30	40	50
10	20	30	40	50

A Place for Poetry

When Mrs. Olinski first started teaching, Margaret Draper (Diamondstein) was the principal. Margaret Draper required all sixth graders to memorize at least 14 lines of poetry each month. Hold a Poetry Memorization Month in your classroom. Bring in several examples of poetry books for students to use as resources. You may want to include some from the list below:

Kock, K. *Wishes, Lies, and Dreams*. (Vintage, 1970)

Prelutsky, J. *A Pizza the Size of the Sun*. (Greenwillow, 1996)

Silverstein, Shel. *Where the Sidewalk Ends*. (Harper and Row, 1974)

Sword, Elizabeth Hauge and Victoria McCarthy. *A Child's Anthology of Poetry*. (Ecco Press, 1995)

Ask students to memorize a poem of at least 14 lines, or they could memorize two shorter poems that add up to the required lines. Have students present their poems to the class or other classes. Point out these speechmaking tips prior to the students' presentations.

1. Choose a poem that interests you.
2. Make sure you understand the words in the poem and that you can pronounce each word correctly.
3. Make sure you understand the tone of the poem so you will know which words to emphasize.
4. Practice orally. Find someone you can trust to critique your presentation prior to doing it in front of the class.
5. Stand tall and still.
6. Project your voice and talk clearly and at an understandable pace for your audience.
7. Look at your audience, not just your teacher.
8. Avoid unnecessary delays and filler words like "um".
9. Practice to be prepared and confident!

After reading poetry, students could write their own poems that would enhance their understanding of themes found in *The View from Saturday*. They could try one or more of the poetry forms listed below.

1. Acrostic (word is written vertically to start each line of poetry)
2. Haiku (17 syllables, 3-line poem; 5, 7, 5 syllable pattern)
3. Tanka (31 syllables, 5-line poem;, 5, 7, 5, 7, 7 syllable pattern)
4. Concrete Poem (poem makes a picture with words)
5. Free Verse (any length, non-rhyming no regular meter)
6. Cinquain (unrhymed, 5-line poem)

Line 1: one-word subject
Line 2: two words that describe the subject
Line 3: three words that express action
Line 4: four words that express feeling or emotion
Line 5: one-word synonym for the subject

Unit Test

Matching: Match the quote with the person who said it.

Noah	Izzy Diamondstein	Mr. Singh
Nadia	Julian	Margaret
Ethan	Mrs. Olinski	

1. _____ "Neat," I replied. I hated saying 'neat.' Nadia's red hair in the autumn light made me forget not to say it."
2. _____ "She is Ginger's daughter. Ginger is my dog, and I have given Julian one of her puppies."
3. _____ "I will make each of you a list of what you need. I'll make the list in calligraphy. Watch me, and it will be your first lesson."
4. _____ "By the time they get to sixth grade, honor roll students won't risk making a mistake, and sometimes to be successful, you have to risk making mistakes."
5. _____ "We never carry them to the water . . . . They must walk across their native sand. We think that something registers in their brains that kicks in twenty-five years later because they return to the beach where they were born to lay their eggs."
6. _____ "Think of the atom, Mrs. Olinski. There are energies within that tiny realm that are invisible but produce visible results . . . . Do not feel uneasy, Mrs. Olinski. Hamilton Knapp would truly have been a terrible choice."
7. _____ "Why do you want to go there to see Mr. Walt Disney's Version of the World when you can see Mother Nature's real thing?"
8. _____ "That day, when Gopal told me I had chops, that is the day I would like to live over."

True or False: Write true or false next to each statement below.
1. _____ Nadia's grandfather married Ethan's grandmother.
2. _____ Julian was born and raised in Clarion County at Sillington House.
3. _____ Ethan dreamed of designing costumes and stage sets.
4. _____ Noah rented a tux to be best man in the wedding.
5. _____ Mrs. Olinski was the first teacher at Epiphany Middle School to teach from a wheelchair.

Short Answer: Provide a short answer to each question below.

1. How did Noah get to be best man in Izzy's wedding?
   _____

2. What brought Nadia's grandfather and Margaret Draper together?
   _____

3. What play did Nadia's father get tickets to see?
   _____

4. What books did Julian use to give clues for inviting guests to his party?
   _____

5. How did Mrs. Olinski know Margaret Draper?
   _____

Essay: Answer the following in paragraph form on the back of this sheet.
1. Discuss some of the challenges that Julian faced.
2. How were the Souls different from the other sixth graders at Epiphany Middle School?

Response

Explain the meaning of each of these excerpts from *The View from Saturday*.

Chapter 1:   *"Ladies and gentlemen, will those lucky few who have the specially marked invitations, please come forward. It is time to choose your surprise gift."*

Chapter 2:   *"In the interest of diversity, " she said, "I chose a brunette, a redhead, a blond, and a kid with hair as black as print on paper."*

Chapter 3:   *"A puzzle!" Julian exclaimed. "I love puzzles. Let's do it now."*

Chapter 4:   *"Your son has something growing out of his head," I said as I pulled two bacon-shaped doggie treats from his ears. "I think these belong to you..."*

Chapter 5:   *"Furthermore," Mrs. Olinski added, "sometimes we even have to risk making fools of ourselves."*

Chapter 6:   *"Now, Mr. Knapp and Mr. Lord," she said, "I would like the two of you to teach the entire class how to belch on command. Please describe the process for all of us."*

Chapter 7:   *"With all due respect, sir, you are wrong."*

Chapter 8:   *"No, Mr. Singh, I'm afraid I don't. Is this some sort of strange Indian philosophy, Mr. Singh? Reincarnation. That sort of thing?"*

Chapter 9:   *"And * where * did * we * get * all * these * bee-YOU-tee-ful * red * curls?"*

Chapter 10: *Mr. Singh replied, "It is a skill he learned when he lived on the cruise ship, Mrs. Olinski. He learned to be a passenger. He learned to read the ocean by the cupful. He also learned to regard each port of call as part of the journey and not as the destination. Every voyage begins when you do."*

Chapter 11:   *"Kindness, yes, Mrs. Olinski. Noah, Nadia, and Ethan found kindness in others and learned how to look for it in themselves."*

Chapter 12: *She waited until they were all in their usual places, and then she asked, "Did I choose you or did you choose me?"*

Conversation

Work in size-appropriate groups to write or perform the conversations that might have occurred in each of the following situations.

- Noah discusses Century Village with the Souls. (4 persons)

- Nadia tells her mom about Florida. (2 persons)

- Mrs. Olinski talks to Ham and Michael about their actions. (3 persons)

- Julian talks about Epiphany Middle School with his dad. (2 persons)

- Ethan discusses buying the puzzle with his mom. (2 persons)

- Ethan discusses the farmer's market with Mr. Singh. (2 persons)

- Mrs. Olinski talks about her disability with Mr. Singh. (2 persons)

- Mr. Singh talks to Mrs. Olinski about his dreams for his B&B. (2 persons)

- Noah teaches the Souls calligraphy. (4 persons)

- Margaret talks to Nadia about sea turtles. (2 persons)

- Izzy and Margaret talk to Mrs. Olinski about their wedding. (3 persons)

- Ham and Michael discuss the failure of the dog biscuit episode. (2 persons)

- The Souls discuss the competition with Mrs. Olinski. (5 persons)

- The Souls talk about their Eyewitness News experience. (4 persons)

- The Souls talk with two Maxwell students after the competition. (6 persons)

- The Souls talk about their plans for summer vacation. (4 persons)

- Mrs. Olinski talks with Dr. Rohmer about her team. (2 persons)

Bibliography of Related Reading

Fiction:
Beaches
Fox, Paula. *The Village by the Sea.* (Orchard, 1988)
Competitions
Conford, Ellen. *The Luck of Pokey Bloom.* (Simon and Schuster, 1975)
Elish, Dan. *The Worldwide Dessert Contest.* (Orchard, 1988)
Houston, Gloria. *Littlejim.* (Philomel Books, 1990)
Kline, Suzy. *Orp and the Chop Suey Burgers.* (G.P. Putnams, 1990)
Naylor, Phyllis Reynolds. *Beetles, Lightly Toasted.* (Atheneum, 1987)
Peyton, K.M. *Who Sir? Me, Sir?* (Oxford University Press, 1983)
Sebesten, Ouida. *Words by Heart.* (Little Brown, 1979)
Steiner, Barbara. *Dolby and the Woof-Off.* (Morrow Jr., 1991)
Divorce
Abercombie, Barbara. *Cat Man's Daughter.* (Harper and Row, 1981)
Paulsen, Gary. *Hatchet.* (Bradbury, 1987)
Peck, Richard. *Unfinished Portrait of Jessica.* (Delacorte Press, 1991)
Voight, Cynthia. *A Solitary Blue.* (Atheneum, 1983)
Fantasy
Carroll, Lewis. *Alice's Adventure in Wonderland.* (Random, 1988)
Friendship
Adler, Carole S. *Always and Forever Friends.* (Clarion, 1988)
Byars, Betsy. *The Pinballs.* (Harper, 1977)
Greene, Bette. *Phillip Hall Likes Me, I Reckon Maybe.* (Dial, 1974)
Spinelli, Jerry. *Dump Days.* (Little Brown, 1988)
White, Ruth. *Belle Prater's Boy.* (Farrar, Straus, & Giroux, 1996)
Gifted
Fenner, Carol. *Randall's Wall.* (Macmillan, 1991)
Fenner, Carol. *Yolanda's Genius.* (McElderry Books, 1995)
Handicapped
Rabe, Berniece. *Balancing Girl.* (Dutton, 1981)
Jewish holidays
Kaplan, Bess. *The Empty Chair.* (Harper, 1978)
Plays
Perry, George C. *The Complete Phantom of the Opera.* (Holt, 1988)
Schools
Byars, Betsy. *The Burning Question of Bingo Brown.* (Puffin, 1990)
DeClements, B. *Nothing's Fair in Fifth Grade.* (Scholastic, 1981)
Mills, Claudia. *The One and Only Cynthia Jane Thorton.* (Macmillan, 1986)

Naylor, Phyllis Reynolds. *The Agony of Alice.* (Atheneum, 1985)
Pickney, Andrea Davis. *Hold Fast to Dreams.* (Morrow Jr., 1995)
Self-esteem
Blume, Judy. *Blubber.* (Dell, 1974)

Nonfiction:
Animal intelligence
Patent, Dorothy Hinshaw. *How Smart Are Animals?* (Harcourt, Brace, Joanovich,1990)
Calligraphy
Harris, David. *The Art of Calligraphy.* (Kindersley, 1995)
Contests
Pendleton, Scott. *The Ultimate Guide to Student Contests Grade 7–12.* (Walker Publishing Co., 1997)
Divorce
Roxenberg, Maxine B. *Living With a Single Parent.* (Bradbury Press, 1992)
Friendship
Schneider, Meg. *Popularity Has Its Ups and Downs.* (Julian Messner, 1991)
Genealogy
Haley, Alex. *Do People Grow on Family Trees?* Genealogy for Kids and Other Beginners. (Workman Publishers, 1991)
General information
Gale Research. *Webster's Guide to Abbreviations, Acronyms, Initialisms, and Abbreviations.*
Siegel, A. and Margo McLoone Basta. *Information Please Kids' Almanac.* (Houghton Mifflin, 1992)
Jewish holidays
Adler, David A. *The Kid's Catalog of Jewish Holidays.* The Jewish Publication Society, 1996)
Magic
Joyce, Katherine. *Astounding Optical Illusions.* (Sterling, 1994)
Randi, James. *Conjuring.* (St. Martins, 1992)
Sea turtles
Gibbons, Gail. *Sea Turtles.* (Holiday House, 1995)
Patton, Don. *Sea Turtles.* (The Child's World, Inc., 1996)
Theater
Cassady, Marsh. *The Theater and You: A Beginning.* (Meriwether, 1992)

Answer Key

Page 10

1. The competition was held in Albany, New York.
2. The schools that competed were Epiphany Middle School and Maxwell Middle School.
3. A "B & B" letter is a "bread and butter" letter that you write as a short thank-you note.
4. Tillie's cat, T. S., pounced on Noah's lap; Noah jumped up and spilled ink. T. S. walked through the spilled ink and onto five invitations.
5. Mr. Cantor provided orchids for corsages. Tillie made invitations. Mrs. Kerchmer lent African violets for centerpieces. Grandma Sadie made the wedding cake. Rabbi Friedman performed the ceremony. Bella Dubinsky painted a shirt to look like a tuxedo for Noah.
6. Allen Diamondstein tripped on the wagon handle, slid on wet concrete, toppled the wedding cake, hurt his ankle, and was taken away by an ambulance. Noah took his place in the wedding.
7. The five prizes were a hand-painted T-shirt, a calligraphy pen and a bottle of ink, a red wagon, one packet of Post-it Notes, and an orchid plant donated later as the fifth gift (prior to this, the fifth gift was to give up your gift to someone else).
8. Tillie would offer calligraphy lessons to the person who took the pen and ink, and Bella promised fabric painting lessons to the person who took the tuxedo T-shirt.
9. Answers will vary.
10. Answers will vary.

Page 13

1. Shortening $2.30/48 ounces
2. Margarine $1.25/3 lbs.
3. Paper Towels $1.25/160 sheets
4. Brisket $4.45 per lb./2 lbs.
5. Flour $1.55/5 lbs.
6. Ice 17 pounds/$2.29
7. Invitations 25 for $20
8. Pen and ink $1.39 and $3.98
9. Sugar $2.19/5 pounds

Page 15

1. The Souls made Mrs. Olinski feel less timid and less self-conscious about being handicapped.
2. Mrs. Olinski said she chose the four in the interest of diversity.

3. Nadia didn't like her dad hovering over her.
4. When Nadia called her friends, it was hard to get together with them. When they did get together, everyone had changed, so the friendship didn't last.
5. Nadia's best friend is her dog, Ginger.
6. Sea turtles brought Izzy and Margaret together.
7. Margaret would swim and Bubbe would not. Margaret was plump and Bubbe was not.
8. Allen Diamondstein (Nadia's dad) had a client with an extra ticket. He bought it on the spot.
9. Nadia was upset that Margaret arranged for Nadia's mother to have an interview with Dr. Gershom. She was upset that she hadn't been told about it. She was also upset that Margaret was interfering with her life.
10. Nadia's dad planned a trip to Disney World and a stay at a theme hotel. Izzy and Margaret needed help with transporting sea turtles, so Nadia and her dad changed their plans.

Page 20

1. The unwritten rule of the bus was that the seat the students chose on the first day became their permanent seats unless they were so unruly that the bus driver, Mrs. Korshak, made them change seats.
2. Ethan felt he had been a disappointment to his teachers following behind his brother in school. Lucas had been a genius, a star athlete, and a record setter. He was glad Mrs. Olinski was new to the school so she wouldn't have a preconceived notion of what a Potter should be like. Ethan was frustrated about walking in his brother's shadow.
3. Julian wore shorts and knee socks and carried a leather bookbag. No one ever did that.
4. Ethan liked the way the sun made fringes of Nadia's hair and framed her face like a halo.
5. Julian probably did not write "cripple" on the board. Hamilton Knapp looked and smiled at Michael as if they had been up to something. (Accept reasonable answers.)
6. They wrote unkind things on Julian's bookbag. Michael Froelich was planning to knock Julian down at school.
7. He didn't call for help. He reacted strongly and quickly.
8. He dreamed of designing stage sets and costumes.

Answer Key (cont.)

Page 20 (cont.)

9. Ethan and his mom sold pumpkins at the Clarion County Farmer's Market.

10. Julian gave clues to the party on notes. The clues were found in books.

11. Nadia pulled off the longest piece of wallpaper at Sillington House. This awarded her the right to name the team.

12. Answers will vary.

13. Noah—when he was best man in the wedding. Nadia—when she helped Izzy, Margaret, and her dad rescue sea turtles. Ethan—when they had their first tea party. Julian—when he was on a ship sailing back to England.

Page 22

Noah Gershom—teaches calligraphy, was best man in a wedding, and wears glasses

Nadia Diamondstein—is plump, has red-hair, has a dog named Ginger

Julian Singh—has a British accent, wears shorts and knee socks, and has black hair

Mrs. Olinski—is a teacher, a paraplegic, and is cautious about being friendly

Ethan Potter—has blonde hair, his brother is Lucas, dreams of doing theater work

Page 25

1. *Annie*

2. Ginger is the mother of his dog, Alice. Ginger belongs to Nadia. Julian didn't want Michael Froelich to have the honor of having his dog in the play.

3. Ham was going to secretly lace Ginger's dog treats with tranquilizers and laxatives so Ginger would pass out and not be able to perform in the play.

4. They passed each other a penny dated with the year they became the Souls.

5. Julian dropped all the biscuits into Ham's lap. Julian said, "I think these belong to you."

6. Answers will vary.

7. She has to explain how she forms her academic team.

8. Mrs. Olinski almost chose Hamilton Knapp.

9. Mischief is being playful in an irresponsible way, and malice is an intent to injure or cause distress.

10. Mrs. Olinski liked what she saw—four children showing each other courtesy, enjoying each other's company, and acting unselfishly.

11. Julian didn't seem like a team player. He was just his own person—"an island unto himself."

Pages 27, 28, and 29

Answers will very. Accept reasonable responses.

Page 30

1. The advisory panel could not find a reference for the word, "tip." "Posh," was also a problem, but they approved that word more quickly.

2. The Souls were a sixth-grade team who beat the seventh-grade and eighth-grade teams. They worked from the bottom up to the top.

3. Dr. Rohmer was risking that Mr. Fairbain would be embarrassing to the school by mispronouncing words. He had done this in the past.

4. They met for tea every Saturday.

5. Mr. Singh said things to Mrs. Olinski that she had never made public to anyone.

6. The Bible is the category.

7. The Souls' and Mrs. Olinski's comments were never aired— only Mr. Fairbain's comment that the taxpayers would be proud which was spoken at an awkward time.

8. Bella Dubinsky designed T-shirts. Five hundred were printed and sold to help pay team expenses.

9. The Souls wanted to receive the trophy with Mrs. Olinski.

10. The trophy was called "The Loving Cup." Accept reasonable answers why.

11. Mrs. Olinski would no longer have the preparation and interaction that the competition offered once it ended.

Page 31

1. *Alice in Wonderland*
2. bottoms up
3. break a tie
4. after school
5. 4 o'clock
6. wins over losses
7. taken out on a stretcher
8. round of applause
9. high overhead
10. half credit
11. two reasons
12. balancing act
13. showdown
14. add up to a loss
15. road in silence
16. 4-part question
17. invisible
18. 8th grade
19. charge admission
20. reincarnation

Answer Key *(cont.)*

Page 32

aka—	also known as
AP—	1. American Plan 2. Associated Press
APO—	army post office
AIDS—	acquired immunodeficiency syndrome
BSA—	Boy Scouts of America
CIA—	1. Central Intelligence Agency 2. Culinary Institute of America
CD—	1. compact disc 2. certificate of deposit 3. Civil Defense
CPR—	cardiopulmonary resuscitation
DDS—	doctor of dental surgery
EXT.—	1. extension 2. exterior 3. external 4. extra 5. extract
E-mail—	electronic mail
ESL—	English as a Second Language
FBI—	Federal Bureau of Investigation
FDA—	Food and Drug Administration
GED—	1. General Educational Development 2. General Equivalency Diploma
HS—	high school
MADD—	Mothers Against Drunk Drivers
NASA—	National Aeronautics and Space Administration
NBA—	1. National Boxing Association 2. National Basketball Association
PGA—	Professional Golfer's Association
POSH—	port out, starboard home
P.S.—	1. postscript 2. public school
PTA—	Parent-Teacher Association
SAT—	1. Saturday 2. Scholastic Aptitude Tests 3. saturate (ed, ion)
UPC—	Universal Product Code
UPI—	United Press International
WPM—	words per minute
WW—	World War
WWW—	World Wide Web
XS—	extra small

Page 33

1. M	6. A	11. C	16. F
2. G	7. N	12. D	17. Q
3. L	8. P	13. I	
4. J	9. B	14. E	
5. O	10. K	15. H	

Page 42

Matching

1. Ethan
2. Nadia
3. Noah
4. Mrs. Olinski
5. Margaret
6. Mr. Singh
7. Izzy Diamondstein
8. Julian

True-False

1. true
2. false
3. true
4. false
5. true

Short Answer

1. Noah was best man in Izzy's wedding because someone needed to replace Allen Diamondstein who hurt his ankle and couldn't walk down the aisle.
2. Sea turtles brought Izzy and Margaret together.
3. Nadia's father got tickets to *The Phantom of the Opera*.
4. Julian used *Alice's Adventure in Wonderland* and a world atlas.
5. Margaret Draper was the principal at the elementary school where Mrs. Olinski first taught.

Essay

1. Accept reasonable answers that are supported by the book.
2. Accept reasonable answers that are supported by the book.

Page 43

Accept all reasonable responses.

Page 44

Perform the conversations (dramas) in class. Ask students to respond to the conversations in different ways, such as "Are the conversations realistic?" or "Are the words the characters are saying in keeping with their personalities?"